Try It and S

Written by: Janet Kuester ● Illustrated by: Amanda Michelle Lee Cruz

The Ninja Connection

The Music Connection
10751 165th Street
Orland Park, IL 60467

Try It and See
Text copyright 2018 by Janet Kuester
Illustrations copyright 2018 Amanda Michelle Lee Cruz

This Special Book Belongs to

_____

Once upon a time there was a little girl named Janice.

One day, her Grandma and Grandpa took her to a cartoon movie. Her Mommy was busy with Janice's little brother and sister, so Grandma and Grandpa wanted Janice to have a special time with them. It was her 5th birthday.

The cartoons were beautiful but as she watched the movie all Janice could do was listen to the beautiful music.

When she got home she and Daddy watched Saturday morning cartoons. She heard the beautiful music again.

A few days later, she asked the grownups about the music.

"Oh," Grandma said as they baked cookies together, "You like classical music!"

That Christmas, Grandma bought a recording for Janice. It was called "Swan Lake". She and her sister Marie danced to it and pretended to ice skate.

Dad and Mom noticed that Janice wanted to play music. They bought her little musical toys: a pretend piano and a little accordion.

Her little brother Adam had gotten a toy xylophone that made music as they pulled it. Janice liked this musical toy the best because the tone was the best. She began to pick out some simple tunes.

Several years passed.

At school, Mrs. White, her 2nd grade teacher loved to sing with the children. She played the piano.

"How does she know what note to play? "Janice wondered as she watched Mrs. White. Mrs. White was looking at a music book that had notes and words on the page.

Janice decided that she wanted to play the piano! Then she would be able to play all the songs she heard and make up her own too!

She came home and told Mommy, "I want to play piano."

Are you sure," Mommy asked? "Pianos cost a lot of money.

You would have to practice every day."

Mommy and Janice went to the music school that was a mile from home.

"Janice wants to take piano, but I would like to find out more," she said.

The woman at the music school office, Miss Pat, was very kind. She told Mommy about "Try It and See" class. "Janice can try the 5 instruments we recommend for children 5-7 years for an early start, she said.

Miss Pat turned to Mommy. "And you will come with Janice to class too so you can watch her try the instruments. "She whispered to Janice, "Mommy will be your practice partner: she will remind you to practice and help you."

After Mommy heard about all the different instruments, she decided to enroll Janice in "Try It and See".

"Janice, she said, "You will get to try all of the instruments and then we can decide together which one will be the best option.

First was piano. Janice loved it! Mr. Andrew and Miss Jessica taught the children Hot Cross Buns and Mary Had a Little Lamb the first day with just one finger!

Next came violin: the children learned how to pluck a string and a beginning bow hold.

Miss Anna made it so much fun!

Cello was next ! It was big and made a deep sound . Mr. James showed them some beautiful and funny sounds a cello could make.

The guitar was next! The instructor, Mr. Jack, made it look easy. The sound of the strummed strings was beautiful.

Finally, drums were next. What loud sounds the children made! Miss Maryanne taught them some rhythms.

It was the last class. Mommy asked: "Which one, Janice?"

"The piano!" "I want to play the piano!"" I love the sound!"

There was a notice on the school bulletin board for a used piano at a great price, so Mommy and Daddy bought the piano.

Janice took lessons. Practicing was easy. Every day, Janice got up before school and practiced her songs. She got a sticker when her songs were mastered.

When she got older she helped little children in the neighborhood practice. She also took up the violin at school. Lessons on violin at the music school soon followed.

At church, they needed a pianist to play hymns and she did that too.

Janice grew up and kept playing music every day. She played in orchestra; she accompanied students, she found a partner and performed piano four hands.

She went to college. She grew up and got married.

She had 2 children who learned to play music too.

She decided that she also wanted to teach little children and help them learn to play music

to express what was in their heart too.

So, she started a music school and lived happily ever after teaching playing, and being with musicians, friends and little boys and girls who loved music as much as her and encouraging them to:

"Try It and See!"

The End

Made in United States
Orlando, FL
21 June 2023

34382963R00033